Foreword

Good news, ladies and gentlemen. The grey sc   -tailed "Nutkin" image. Even some of the most fervent   s have had to concede that to allow such a dominant no..   ood is insanity. The motive for writing this book is the recent announcement ajesty's Government that it intends to fund a National cull of the non-native grey squirrel, *Sciurus carolinensis*. This is an unprecedented move towards common-sense wildlife management and the only example I can recall in my generation. Not since the East-Anglian coypu cull of the 1950's has HMG sponsored total eradication of a species. The reasons are there for all to see. Not just the estimated £10 million of damage to forestry but also its unchallengeable contribution to the decline of our native red squirrel, *Sciurus vulgaris*. A lively, inquisitive and entertaining creature ... the grey squirrel will now always have a foothold and food source in our towns and cities. For this reason alone, a national cull is probably doomed to failure. In rural areas, however, the air-rifle hunter will always find work to do and landowners asking for a reduction in numbers. It is the fifth most unpopular resident on a farmers or foresters estate, behind the fox, the rabbit, the rat and the wood-pigeon. On the foresters estate, it is second only to deer on the 'nuisance' list. Despite the overwhelming evidence, many conservationists continue to imitate the ostrich and claim that songbird nest predation by *Sciurus carolinensis* is negligible ... but we know different, don't we? All genuine country folk know. Moves to eradicate the grey and re-establish our native red squirrel are building in momentum throughout the UK and this is giving opportunity not just to trappers but also air rifle hunters. For the adept air rifle hunter has a very effective, safe and non-disruptive tool for clearing grey squirrels. I know, because I cull hundreds every year. Becoming adept is all about knowing how, where and when to tackle this abundant and challenging quarry. Hopefully, this book will help both novice and experienced shooter with it's tips and insights into grey squirrel behaviour.

Disclaimer

In offering this work to the reader, the author does not guarantee in any way that the reader will achieve the level of success in shooting he enjoys. Many factors contribute to the development of a successful hunter and shooter ... practise, experience, field-craft, determination and dedication. This book simply shares the factors, the behaviour and the experience of a hunter / writer who has enjoyed a lifetime of squirrel control with a rifle. The author wishes you equal success with your own squirrel hunting but in no way underwrites that buying this book will guarantee it.

Any reference to hunting, animal welfare and national law in this book are based on current UK legislation. The author will not be held responsible for any misinterpretation of the content

All text, photographs and illustrations in this work were created and supplied by the author and remain his copyright.

© Ian Barnett 2015

The Invasion

Although small colonies of greys squirrels were reported as introduced to estates in Denbighshire and Montgomeryshire in the early 1800's these were believed to have failed to survive. The first real culprit responsible for the introduction of *Sciurus Carolinensis* from it's native North America was a certain Mr T.V.Brocklehurst who released a pair into the wild at Henbury Park in Cheshire in 1876. It has to be assumed that they bred successfully as within eight years a pair was recorded as shot at Highfields in Nottinghamshire, thirty plus miles away. Five years after Brocklehursts innocent introduction to the North, a certain Mr G.S. Page set five greys free in Bushey Park, Middlesex. These failed to survive. A year later Mr Page imported ten more from America and released them at the Duke of Bedford's seat, Woburn Abbey. Interestingly, the same estate that unleashed both muntjac deer and Chinese water deer on the UK! By 1920 these had populated an area more than 1000 square miles around Woburn. To make things worse, grey squirrels became 'fashionable' to have on your country pile and soon Woburn greys were being trapped and released all over Britain (and Ireland). These populations soon spread, estimated at a rate of a dozen square miles per year. In Scotland, introductions made in 1892 spread equally as fast. By the early 1930's there were an estimated 10,000 square miles of grey squirrel territory across Britain and Ireland. In 1931 they were beset by a disease which became an epidemic and all but wiped out colonies across several counties. They bounced back with a venom and by 1937 the Authorities realised that it's bad habits and impact on our native red squirrel needed checking.

A red squirrel

A Grey Squirrel Prohibition of Importation and Keeping Act was issued. This made it illegal to import the grey from abroad or keep one as a pet. Alas, too little, too late. Incidentally, this Act is still in force. In 1953 a bounty was set on grey squirrel tails (and free cartridges offered) by the Forestry Commission and Ministry of Agriculture. This was set at one shilling (10p. Though the bounty was later doubled, about £100,000 was paid out by 1958 when the scheme was stopped. In 1980, Keith Laidler reported in his excellent book 'Squirrels In Britain' that there were still areas in Wales, Lancashire, Cumbria, Essex, Suffolk and Norfolk which were free of grey squirrels. Sadly, 25 years later, that doesn't remain the case. In Norfolk, where I now live, few but the eldest residents remember the numerous red squirrels that cavorted in the county's rich forestry. There are now an estimated two and a half million grey squirrels in the UK now. Sadly, it is estimated by the Forestry Commission that less than one hundred thousand red squirrels remain in Britain as I write this … and these remaining are under dire pressure as the grey continues to bully its way through their remaining territories.

An increasingly rare sight in Britain

Natural History

Legend has it that a squirrel was present in the Garden of Eden and was so traumatised at seeing the love-making of Adam and Eve that it fluffed up its tail and wrapped it around its eyes in bashful embarrassment! God was so pleased at its piousness, He made the bottle-brush tail a permanent feature. We hunters can be grateful to The Almighty for this generosity, as that bottle-brush tail is often the first indicator of hidden quarry. As for piousness? The grey squirrel is very promiscuous and is often seen racing around the British wood on a flirtatious 'catch-me-if-you-can' mating game. In reality, the grey squirrel has all the morality and piousness of the average rock star!

The name for the genus, *sciurus*, is derived from two Greek words. *Skia*, meaning shadow and *oura*, meaning tail. Shadow-tail, no doubt linked to the squirrels habit of covering itself coyly with its bushy tail.

Grey squirrels can be found almost anywhere on mainland Britain where there are woods and forest. They will build their dreys in almost any tree .. deciduous or conifer. If you shoot territory without any trees, then I'm sorry. You won't see any squirrels! To find them feeding, simply look for food-bearing trees such as oak, hazel, beech or pine.

The grey squirrels body is about 25/30cm long and its bushy tail is nearly as long again. A mature adult weighs in at about half a kilogramme. They are a rodent, with a similar bone, skull and jaw structure to the rat, hence they are often referred to as 'tree rats'.

A grey squirrel

The grey squirrels nest is called a 'drey' or in some areas, a 'jug'. It is a woven dome of twigs from broad-leaved deciduous trees, lined with softer materials such as moss, feather and leaves. In summer this is usually built high in a tree but in winter built within a cleft near the trunk. The greys nest, when the leaves die, takes on the look of a scruffy ball of brown leaves. The red squirrels drey is usually built in conifer trees such as pine or larch and tends to be a much tidier dome. The drey is used as shelter from predators and poor weather, a night bed and as the breeding nest for the female. In suburban areas dreys can often be built in household roofs or, worse still, in attics or thatch. Squirrels inside the house are a recipe for disaster as, like the brown rat, they can chew through pipes and cables.

A grey squirrel drey in winter

The grey squirrels diet is primarily vegetarian. It's favourite food is undeniably the acorn (which is why oak trees are a prime place to target them). It also eats beech-mast, pine seeds, hazel nuts, walnuts, conkers, flower bulbs, maize cobs and sweet chestnuts. Greys, like reds, also eat fungi. Extra nutrients are taken by tree-barking, stripping the bark from tree trunks to get to saps which are rich in water and mineral salts. Greys are also partial to eggs and chicks in spring (see Bad Habits). Food is sourced via smell, a fact that becomes very apparent when you watch them recover winter caches of acorns from beneath leaf mulch and snow.

Greys, like most mammals, use marking sites to communicate territory, presence and breeding condition. Unfortunately this, too, includes bark stripping. The males use urine and musk from glands to mark. Passing females leave a mark which will tell the male when they are ready to mate. Breeding occurs twice a year .. usually around February and July. The female produces three or four 'kits' after a 44 day gestation period. This is an important point for the hunter (see

Tips). The young will be reach independence within about 12 weeks and females can breed at around 10 to twelve months old.

Grey squirrels move around their territory using a series of well established forest paths and aerial highways . The times of their movement and direction of travel can be very predictable, particularly when raiding food sources such as game feeders or bird tables. This habitual behaviour makes hunting them easier for the shooter who takes time to simply sit and watch for a while. Activity and behaviour changes with the seasons. During warmer months, greys tend to be most active for a couple of hours after dawn. They take a siesta while the sun is at its highest, then appear again for the last couple of hours of the day. In winter, they wait for the dreys to warm, therefore they are most active during the middle of the day.

Contrary to popular belief, grey squirrels <u>do not</u> hibernate in winter. Squirrels may retire for long periods (into the dreys) in inclement weather but they still come out regularly to feed and forage.

Incidentally there is a slightly larger, more aggressive melanistic (black) strain of squirrel in some Southern counties. They are particularly prevalent around the public parks in Letchworth, Hertfordshire but appear to have spread to other counties in the South Midlands too.

Bad Habits

The grey squirrel has become rural enemy number one in recent years for good reason. Its relentless bark-stripping and nest raiding have put it firmly on the list of a "shoot-on-sight" species. Foresters, farmers and country folk have all evidenced its danger to tree cultivation and to resident songbird species. On shooting estates, predation of game-bird nests makes it intolerable. In some areas, local culls have been authorised (particularly to protect breeding sanctuaries for red squirrels) and the call for a national pogrom comes as no surprise.

So what about this estimated £10 million worth of damage to forestry annually? Grey squirrels attack the primary shoots of newly sprouted trees on plantations, which are rich in protein. Even when they don't kill the sapling, it will grow misshapen and become a commercially worthless timber. The most serios crime, however, is indiscriminate 'barking' of trees. This involves stripping significant sections of bark from mature trees, usually over ten years old. Not to eat the bark itself but to extract nutrients and water from the exposed softer cambial wood beneath. Barking is usually done in late spring or early summer and where ring-barking (removing the bark from right around the trunk) occurs, the wood above the ring will die. The leaves are unable to photosynthesise as they have no water, so no food travels back down the trunk to sustain its life. Open wounds on a deciduous tree from bark removal can heal, but many are attacked by fungi, weakening the timber and leaving it susceptible to storm damage.

Bark Stripping

Never under-estimate the grey squirrels penchant for fresh songbird, game-bird and pigeon eggs or young chicks. Squirrels are omnivorous and are highly adept, curious, athletic climbers and jumpers. They will reach any food they set their sights on, we've all seen the 'Mission Impossible' type documentaries. The nickname 'tree-rat' is used often and, in my opinion, justified. Like the brown rat, they have little fear when feeding. On the ground they will boldly evict a bird as large as a pheasant and they will strip a pheasant or partridge nest of eggs within ten minutes. Greys will even tackle the nests of aggressive birds like the jay, hence they are mortal enemies. They are also a visible nuisance around bird tables, cleverly raiding feeders and seed left out for songbirds, bullying the birds away.

The grey rarely physically attacks the red squirrel, though this has been documented. Although both greys and reds have a bi-annual breeding cycle, similar sized litters and compete for the same food and territory ... it was inevitable that the larger, more aggressive grey squirrel would push the red squirrel close to extinction in this country. One of the main reasons, however, has been because the grey squirrel is a vector for the squirrel parapox virus (SQPV, see separate chapter) to which it is largely immune but which is lethal to the more fragile red squirrel.

Pheasant eggs on a squirrel 'table'

In many urban areas and parks, the grey squirrel is adored by the public. Perhaps understandably as it is a wild creature freely available for viewing by the public and in many cases, the only wild animal many children will get to see. Yet parkland and public spaces house few, if any, of the grey squirrels natural predators so they thrive unchecked. They lose their timidity and are so approachable that many can be hand-fed (so not wild in my eyes!). It will be interesting to see how Her Majesty's Government and Local Authorities approach a request to cull these parkland animals and ... if they do ... how they tackle the job under the gaze of a distressed and protesting public? Of course, if they don't get culled too, these enclaves will be the breeding ground for the re-emergence of the grey squirrel in rural areas.

Ever alert and searching for food

Pheasant egg cleaned out by a grey squirrel

Natural Predators

In mainland UK, the grey squirrel only has two serious ground predators .. the fox and the domestic cat. They are usually nimble enough, though, to escape such large prey. In Scotland, the wild cat is a threat but with their own numbers so low, hardly a serious one. Pine martens, being adept climbers are a serious threat and apparently relentless in their pursuit of a scented squirrel. Stoats will often raid dreys to take kits but I doubt they would tackle the parents. Few people realise that stoats can climb nimbly but I have not only found pink, blind kits beneath dreys with a classic bite marks on the neck, I have also watched a stoat descend head-first down a pine carrying a young squirrel kit in its jaws. The grey squirrels biggest threat (apart from man) comes from the air in the form of raptors. Goshawks, buzzards, sparrowhawks and owls. In Norfolk I have watched buzzards harassing squirrels in the crowns of tall trees, but have never seen them actually attack and kill a squirrel. They do, however, enjoy the corpses I often leave on the midden pile!

The common buzzard

When attacked, the squirrels three main weapons of defence are its back paws, its teeth and its agility. The grey squirrels bite, as can be imagined from a creature that can break through hazel nuts, is vicious. I've had dogs that have been on the wrong end of a squirrels bite and can testify to that! Before the Hunting Act came into play, of course! Yet another reason to use an air rifle. When chased on the ground it will jink and roll until it makes it to a tree, dash up and often stop to make a quick risk assessment before continuing upwards. If chased by a hawk it will behave completely differently. The squirrel will wind upwards around the trunk, foiling the bird (which can't adjust to such movement).

The grey squirrels biggest threat now, of course, is mankind. Particularly those determined to restore the balance with a restoration of the red squirrel population. Unlike the reds, however, it is unlikely that we will ever see eradication ... just reduction ... of the grey squirrel numbers in the UK.

Author with a cull victim

Squirrel Parapox Virus (SQVP)

Squirrel parapox virus (SQVP) has been identified as one of the major threats to the survival of the British red squirrel. Any red contracting the disease will die a very uncomfortable death with fifteen days. The disease can be treated if caught early enough and it is within the first week that red squirrels (appearing lethargic and docile) are most highly infectious. Grey squirrels can carry the pox virus as a vector with suffering its effects and there is much speculation as to how the relationship between the two species can spread infection. One thing that is apparent is that where colonies of reds and greys co-exist, SQPV spreads through the red population faster until local extinction occurs and the greys move in to colonise the vacuum. The correlation between grey population increase and red extinction is irrefutable. So it is this relationship between imbalance in population that makes a grey squirrel cull essential to the defence of the indigenous red squirrel. This, of course, is not the greys 'fault' yet impossible to ignore.

The symptoms of contagion in reds looks similar to myxomatosis in rabbits (though the two diseases are in no way related). The animal will develop lesions on its toes, legs, genitals, face and eyes. As with myxomatosis, the creature dies a slow lingering death and is vulnerable to predation through weakness and blindness. If found, a diseased red squirrel should be isolated and dispatched for its own good and the good of the species but also reported to a local Red Squirrel Group or a vet.

As direct contact between the two species is rare, the big mystery is how the virus is transferred from grey to red squirrel. Theories include transfer through insect vectors such as flea or ticks, found on both species. It could also be through direct contact with secretions at scenting points while marking territory.

The innocent vector of a virus deadly to our Reds

Know The Law

It is perfectly legal to shoot grey squirrels at any time of the year on land on which you have permission to shoot. That is, land you own or where the owner has asked you to carry out control. There are, however, a number of things to remember to keep you on the right side of the law at all times. So, first of all, who can legitimately use an air rifle? There are age restrictions.

At <u>18 years</u> or older there are no restrictions on buying an air rifle and ammunition, and you can use them wherever you have permission to shoot.

At <u>14-17 years</u> old you can borrow an air rifle and its ammunition. You can also use an air rifle, without supervision, on private premises where you have permission to shoot but … you cannot buy or hire an air weapon, or ammunition, or receive one as a gift. Your air weapon and ammunition must be bought and looked after by someone over 18 … normally your parent, guardian or some other responsible adult. Nor can you have an air weapon in a public place unless you are supervised by somebody aged 21 or over, and you have a reasonable excuse to do so (e.g. while on the way to a shooting ground).

If <u>under 14 years</u> old You can use an air weapon <u>under supervision</u> on private premises with permission from the occupier - normally the owner or tenant. The person who supervises you must be at least 21 years old. You cannot, however, purchase, hire or receive an air weapon or its ammunition as a gift, or shoot, without adult supervision. Parents or guardians who buy an air weapon for use by someone under 14 must exercise control over it at all times, even in the home or garden. *NB. It is illegal to sell an air weapon or ammunition to a person under 18 years of age.*

Other legal aspects to remember include the following:

You may only shoot on land you own or where you have permission from the owner and within its boundaries. This is an important point because if you fire a pellet across the boundary of your land or permitted land, you will commit armed trespass! A crime with serious consequences and harsh penalties. This applies too if you cross over onto un-permitted land (trespass) carrying an air rifle. Even if it is unloaded, you are guilty of armed trespass.

It is an offence to possess an air rifle in a public place without lawful authority or reasonable excuse. Common sense allows that some people may need to travel with a (covered) rifle but carrying permission notes or gun club membership is strongly advised.

It is illegal to discharge your air rifle within 50 feet (16 yards) of the centre of a public highway if, in doing so, you cause someone to be 'injured, interrupted or endangered'. The first one means you're in big trouble anyway. The latter two can include causing drivers or horse-riders to become distracted. So don't wave a gun around near a public highway which, incidentally, includes public footpaths and bridleways.

Why The Air Rifle?

The answer is ... in one simple word ... practicality!

There is absolutely no doubt that trapping squirrels is the most highly effective method of clearing woodland but for many of us, it is totally impractical due to current legislation requiring that traps (both cage and spring traps) need to be checked at least once daily. If, like me, you hold down a day job as well as carrying a bit of voluntary pest control you will never find the time to get around and check these traps to comply with the law. If you do want to consider trapping, I can recommend Steve Caples wonderful book, Trapping and Snaring (Matador ISBN 9781783061679). On the subject of poisoning, I don't like seeing poisons on any wild land, simply because poisoned carrion such a squirrel carcase can be fed on by other wildlife such as buzzards, badgers or owls. Cage-trapped squirrels can be shot or dispatched with a priest. Spring traps normally kill immediately. The air rifle definitely does, in the right hands.

The air rifle is a highly effective tool for grey squirrel control

The modern air rifle is one the safest and most efficient, trouble free tools that can be employed against small vermin. Although much maligned and often associated with teenage thuggery due to a misinformed media, the air rifle is often the gun that every young countryman and woman has cut their shooting teeth on. The single shot, spring piston models of old were the preferred training gun for military cadets across Europe during two World Wars for good reason. The spring powered rifle (or 'springer', as it is often called) automatically teaches solid shooting technique and if you learn to master its recoil, trajectory and trigger technique you will comfortably learn to handle any higher power rifle put in your hands later. Now … having said that, I don't hunt with a springer any more. I use a multi-shot, silenced, pre-charged pneumatic (PCP) air rifle.

The Weihrauch HW100KT multi-shot PCP air rifle

The discharge from a PCP rifle, fitted with a sound moderator (silencer), is nigh on impossible for quarry to hear at ranges over 25 yards. So if you want to cull grey squirrels in numbers, without clearing a wood of quarry with one shot, this is your tool. The shotgun is fine if you are drey-poking (explained later) but in general hunting terms, one shot and you've sent every other squirrel into cover. The .22LR rimfire rifle is as effective as the air rifle but (even with a sound moderator) too noisy. Most of your shots at squirrels will be elevated (shooting upwards) so the rimfire is a potentially dangerous tool for squirrel control without solid back-stops. So, for me (on my shooting permissions), the rim-fire is a no-no.

The British legal limit for unlicensed air rifles is an output power less than 12 foot pounds (12 ft/lbs). Any rifle which emits greater power than this is classified as a Section One firearm and requires a Firearms Certificate (FAC). Air rifle manufacturers do produce higher power rifles. I own two myself and have an FAC. I rarely use them. These are rifles that bridge the gap between the legal limit air rifle and the .22LR or .177HMR rimfires. They are useful on rabbits, corvids et al when there is little cover and you need to shoot from a distance. They are also useful for brown hare control when required, but I have found them totally useless for grey squirrel control due to over-penetration (see next chapter).

Nearly 40 years of squirrel hunting, the last 10 with a PCP, has convinced me that the sub 12 ft/lb PCP air rifle is the right tool for the job. You have to stalk closer, so the hunting is genuine ... you have to have fieldcraft skills to do the job ... and you are giving the squirrel fair law. So it makes for a creditable field-sport. It makes ambushing rabbits or roost-shooting pigeons seem like potting fish in a barrel (and rabbits or pigeons aren't that easy to shoot!). Not for me the swinging shotgun and the driven bird ... which is not 'hunting'. Nor the randomness of the deer stalk (though I would cherish the meat). I can hunt squirrels all year around with no 'seasons'. I can use them for corvid bait, eat them myself, supply the tails to fly-fisherman or feed the local buzzards to keep them off the game-bird poults.

The grey squirrel is a formidable and ever-present pest in British woodland or forest. It shouldn't be here, but it is. There are thousands of air-rifle users (and prospective hunters) who, given the mandate, could be on the front line of grey squirrel control on behalf of the native red squirrel if landowners simply trust us and give us permission.

Squirrel tails are highly prized by fly fishermen for fly-tying

A quarry for all seasons

Which Calibre?

If you're looking to choose an air rifle, the first problem you will encounter is choosing which calibre to use. Most rifles are available in the two main calibres, .177 and .22, and if you seek advice from other shooters you will soon find that loyalty to a particular calibre is as fierce as the rivalry between football supporters. The .177 versus .22 argument has raged for decades. So what do I favour? Over most of my four decades as an air rifle hunter I had always favoured the .22 calibre rifle and pellet, convinced that the larger pellet gives more of killer 'clout' when it engages with quarry. The sacrifice for using the heavier pellet is a deeper trajectory. Put very simply the .177 pellet travels faster and flatter than the .22 pellet. That makes the .177 more 'forgiving' to the shooter in terms of accuracy but I've always argued that an expert, accurate shooter doesn't need 'forgiveness'! When I started writing for airgun magazines ten years ago, I was duty-bound to try the .177 calibre a number of times and hated the calibre. As a full-on hunter (not a target shooter) I just find the small pellet far too inclined to over-penetrate (often passing through quarry like pigeons and crows). This usually results in injury, not death. I am a highly ethical hunter and I demand a clean kill. So .177, no sorry, not for me.

Please note that at the start of the last paragraph I said "over most of four decades"? Just to confuse the reader further, there is a 'middle' calibre available on some rifles. The .20 calibre. A year ago I was challenged by a magazine reader to try it, having tried .177 again and having discounted it once again. Somewhat cynically, I admit, I agreed to take part in a six month hunting experiment with a .20 rifle and pellet combination on behalf of Airgun Shooter magazine, whom I write for monthly. Within two months, realising that I had a 100% kill rate with the slightly smaller pellet, I was converted. More importantly, with respect to this book, it is a lethal grey squirrel calibre. Let me expand on that.

The .22 versus the .20 pellet

To shoot and cleanly dispatch a grey squirrel you have two options with regard to what hunters call the 'kill zone'. The brain and the heart/lung areas. There is a quite ridiculous (in my opinion) school of thought within air rifle hunting circles that culling should be via head-shots only. Having shot squirrels very effectively for nearly 40 years I favour the heart/lung shot on squirrels. The grey squirrel has a skull like a walnut, protecting a tiny (yet intelligent) brain. It also has a very compact engine room (the heart/lung area) tucked behind the shoulder. A correctly placed pellet in all three calibres will penetrate that wall of bone (the skull) or the softer rib area and shut down the squirrels vital systems swiftly. Yet the effectiveness will change according to the distance between gun and squirrel. I find, in reality, that I shoot most squirrels at ranges between ten to thirty yards. Both .22 and .20 pellets will implode at these distances and expand within the skull or heart and deliver a swift kill. In .177, however, I would be reluctant to take a head shot at ten or fifteen yards and definitely not a body shot for fear of the pellet passing straight through. Again, however, I am generalising because choice of pellet is important too!

There are many fancy, best thing since sliced bread, pellet variations. Trust an old hunter and stick to the good old dome-headed, skirted lead 'diablo' pellet for squirrels. They are designed to flatten on impact, delivering the ballistic shock needed to shut down either the 'engine room' or the nervous system.

So, in summary of the previous two chapters, my recommendation for successful grey squirrel control is a legal-limit multi-shot PCP air rifle in either .20 (which can be rare) or .22 calibre using diablo pellets. I use a Weihrauch 100KT rifle with H&N FTT pellets in both calibres and have shot thousands of grey squirrels over the past ten years with this sort of combination. For this reason, all other chapters of this book assume you have taken my advice and are using a PCP air rifle.

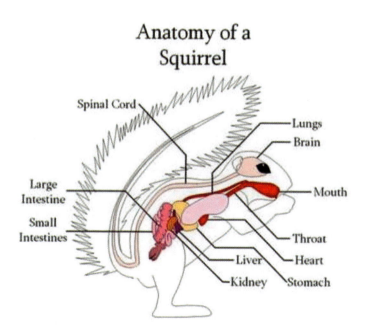

The Telescopic Sight

The perfect compliment to the PCP rifle is the telescopic site (scope). In fact, you would find it hard to buy a PCP with old fashioned open-sights and rightly so. Vermin control demands respect for quarry and the scope allows you to bring the quarry's profile much closer to you so that you pick the kill zone for a clean dispatch and minimise risk of injury to the creature. So which scope is the best to use and how do you fit it and zero it?

Like your choice of rifles, your choice of scope is immense. Like rifles, you get what you pay for. Cheap rifles and cheap scopes will just result in future grief. My advice is to buy the best rifle you can afford (push that a bit, but don't tell your partner!) and buy a scope roughly half the value of your rifle. Good quality optics make for high quality shooting, so don't compromise.

When choosing a scope you need to consider size and reticule type. Again, this may be dictated by budget. The squirrel hunter often operates in low light conditions (amongst trees and under a shaded canopy). A lens with a wide objective lens (that's the fat lens at the silencer end of the scope!) of 40mm or ... better still 50mm ... will capture more light and even enhance vision in low light conditions. Personally I use scopes made by Hawke Optics, who offer a range of different reticule types. I favour (on a British legal-limit rifle) the Nite-Eye scope and the SR6 reticule. The legendary 'Xmas tree'. At 6x magnification it provides a very clear visual map for both distance shots and elevated shots. If you use it with Hawkes own free-to-download ballistic calculation software (Chairgun and Hawke BRC) you can build (and print) reticule maps which you can carry in your pocket until you have mentally memorised them. The reason I favour the Nite-Eye is that it has an IR reticule option (a coloured reticule in either red or green) which is useful in poor light conditions where a standard black reticule is hard to see.

Whatever your choice, a scope with parallax adjustment is a 'must'. Don't ask me to explain parallax, it's too boring to contemplate, but put simply you need to be able to wind the objective lens to focus on the approximate distance you will be shooting at. At legal-limit, this is easy. Trust me. Just set your distance gauge to about 28 yards. You will be able to see everything from 10 to 50 yards clearly enough to make the shot.

At the other end of the scope is the ocular lens. Make sure you pick a scope with an adjustable one. If you wear specs or contact lenses, you will need to use this lens to fine-tune the 'crispness' of vision through the scope. This is also the end where you dial in magnification ratios. Again, trust me. Dial to 6x (vital on an SR6 reticule). The temptation to wind-up the magnification and see your quarry at 12x mag or more brings problems. It will acutely expose your 'shaking' while lining up the shot and reduce your confidence. Dial to 6x, zero at 6x and leave it there, always.

Of course, a scope is useless until you've zeroed it in. The legal limit air rifle has a widely arced trajectory at any calibre, due to the low power. Don't let that low power put you off, however. It's still more than enough to kill small vermin cleanly. Take a look at this graph from the Hawke Optics Chairgun programme:

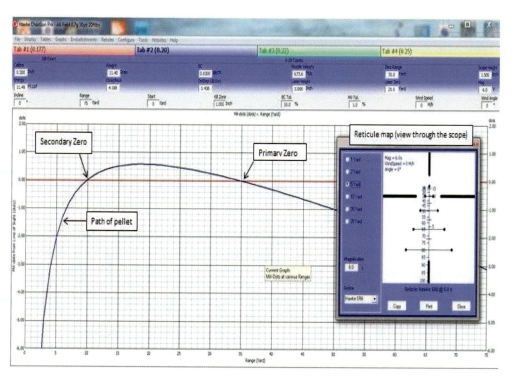

What it shows is that as the pellet exits the barrel it drops first but as it gathers speed it rises, passes through a point we call secondary zero (in this case 11 yards), continues to rise, then drops through what we term primary zero (30 yards) and falls away over distance as it loses momentum and gravity takes its toll. This path is called 'trajectory' and you can see that it is very important to learn how this affects accuracy before placing a shot. If your quarry is between 11 and 30 yards (perfect zero) you need to place the cross-hair slightly under the quarry kill zone as you look through the scope. If the quarry is below 11 yards away or over 30 yards away you need to place the cross-hair above the quarry kill zone at varying degrees, according to distance. This is where the reticule map on the right is useful, as you can see. It tells you exactly where to place your cross-hair at a given distance.

So all you need to do now is learn how to judge range! More on that later. Please note that you need to learn to judge windage too. This is the horizontal adjustment you need to make to allow for the effect of wind or breeze on the travelling pellet.

So, in summary. I favour a Hawke Nite-Eye SR6 IR 3-12 x 50mm scope dialled into 28yards and at 6x mag.I have shot thousands of grey squirrels in all light conditions with these scopes.

Shooting Basics

One thing I must make clear here is that you can't learn to shoot by reading about it. It's like driving a car. You need to be behind the wheel to gain confidence and understand what you need to do to make the car go in the direction you want and within your control. It's the same with a rifle. You need to pick up a rifle and practise like hell. All I can do in a short book like this is impart some of the experience I have in using air rifles.

The simple act of executing a rifle shot can be as auto-responsive as changing gears in a car once you've learnt the sequence of *'see quarry, judge range, sight-up, arm the rifle and shoot'*. With practise, the sequence becomes second nature, a series of physical and mental actions that need little analysis unless things are going badly wrong. Advising the reader on how to achieve this process is very difficult to do on the written page. Not that I profess to be the ideal teacher either! What I do know, though, is my own marksmanship has developed through constant practise (not on a shooting range but out in the field and wood). Not on live quarry, but on inanimate objects like crab apples, pine cones, conkers or stones on fence-posts. When you learn to shoot random targets at varying distances and angles, you are learning how to shoot quarry. Your average grey squirrel isn't going to oblige you by sitting at exactly 30 yards on the level (the point to which you've zeroed your rifle). It will be further or closer. It will be down in a hollow or high in a tree. Learning how to deal with these scenarios is part of the shooters apprenticeship and … trust me … is better achieved in the field.

Learn to shoot on static targets, not live ones

One of the key shortcuts to success in hunting with an air rifle is to pick one gun, one scope, the pellet your barrel favours for accuracy ... and stick with them! I see too many hunters chop and change, always blaming the kit they use for poor performance. Bruce Lee once said 'Fear not the man who has learned a thousand kicks. Fear the man who has practised one kick a thousand times'. The shooter who uses one rifle, one scope and one pellet type will master the execution of accurate, clean kills swiftly and consistently.

When we talked about scopes earlier, I mentioned that you need to master the art of visual range-finding. Judging a reasonably accurate distance from muzzle to quarry is imperative. Your average squirrel won't sit there tolerantly and pose for you to use a digital range-finder. Your mental judgement needs to be made inside a second or two. There is no better way to do this than 'live it' in everything you do. Measure your average stride (I'm a short-arse so mines almost exactly a yard). Pace out your day, whatever you do. How many paces from the lamp post to the post box? How long from one end of the office suite to the other. The distance to the fence post from where you're standing? Keep challenging yourself. Turn that around on itself. Place a pine cone or a small stone (the size of a squirrels head) on a fence post and walk away 25 paces. Turn around and attempt to shoot it within 5 seconds. Try the same at 15, 30, 40 yards. Test your ragnge finding competence against your shooting competence. That's how you learn to shoot accurately and hunt live quarry with justification. Practice on random targets first. Ensure you need a protractor and compasses to quantify range. This is the real world. It's wild and sometimes you'll get it wrong ... but when you do, you'll be even more eager to get it right! When you can snatch up an air rifle and drop a conker from a tree at 35 yards, elevated, you will never worry again about shooting at a squirrel in a tree top.

Learn to shoot elevations by practising on pine cones or conkers

So what about the execution of the shot itself. The sequence should evolve like this. First, mental confirmation that this is a quarry species and that the shot is achievable. If so, bring the gun to your shoulder. Now judge the range, check the angle and that there is a safe backdrop. Do you need to allow for breeze? All this should happen within the first two seconds as you become more adept. Now steady your breathing. The rifle should nestled into your shoulder but not squeezed in tight. Your other hand is holding the fore-stock firmly, but again, not gripping tightly. As you line up the kill zone in the scope, your thumb should flick off the safety-catch instinctively. Take a deep breath and move your index finger into the trigger guard, flat to the trigger blade. Release your breath gently, steady the cross-hair and tickle the trigger. Keep your eye on the quarry until it drops … this is important and is referred to as 'follow-through'. Move your hand from the trigger area to re-cock the rifles side-lever or bolt and (unless a second shot is needed) return the safety catch to 'on'. All of this process should be achievable within 5 seconds when you've learnt to shoot confidently. This is my shooting technique and I'm quite happy with it. You will find, like me, that over-analysis of your technique can have a negative effect on your accuracy.

If you find yourself shooting poorly, check back over the above sequence. Are you breathing in a relaxed way? Suspending your breath right at the moment you shoot will stop the barrel wavering. Watching the pellet fly right through to the target (that 'follow through') stops you snatching back the shot to watch your quarry from over the top of the gun. Hugely important because if you do that, you will often do so before the pellet has exited the barrel … so you've moved the point of impact … unknowingly. Discipline yourself to keep watching through the scope (a good way to achieve this is to get in the habit of re-cocking the rifle with your eye still on the scope).

Another common shooting fault that manifests itself from time to time is 'trigger snatch'. Pulling at the trigger instead of a simple tickle to release the pellet. We often use the term 'pull the trigger' … which we shouldn't really. The pull … or snatch … pulls the barrels alignment slightly and (like the failure to follow through) subtly changes the point of impact (POI). Just a tiny movement at the rifle end can translate to an inch at the quarry end … meaning a miss or (worse still) injury. The proper technique is to use the soft pad of your index finger, horizontal with the trigger blade, to gently tickle it back towards your chin.

Other factors which will affect the shooting sequence are comfort and stance. Comfort is important … warmth, dryness, clothing etc … and will influence how well you take the shot. As for stance, I practise shooting in every conceivable position. My favourite stance, however, will always be the kneeling stance where I can use my thigh as a support for the elbow of the fore-stock arm.

You also need to learn to shoot effectively from a standing (freehand) position when you need to. This will be essential on rough shooting, walk-around sessions on grey squirrels. The new shooter will need to adjust to simply holding the weight of a rifle, particularly shooting it freehand, where the only support is your own arm. This is another reason why I promote 'one-gun' hunting. It's not just about knowing your reticule or rifle intimately, it's also about your muscles being 'educated' to handle the rifle in any situation. Constantly switching guns, will find you struggling with balance and shooting stance. If you stick to one gun, this is less of a problem.

The kneeling stance is my favoured shooting position

But learning to shoot free-hand is essential

If you wear glasses or contact lenses for distance vision, make sure you wear them when shooting. That may seem an obvious statement but it's surprising how many shooters neglect their vision. My father-in-law is a BASC shotgun and safe-shot coach and has learnt over the years that one of his opening questions to a shooter wanting corrective training is "do you wear glasses to drive?" If the answer is "yes" he tells them to put them on and nine times out ten they hit the clays straight away! As a hunter, it beggars belief in my mind how folk think they are going to even see a squirrel, let alone shoot it cleanly, if they don't use the vision correction they use in daily life.

Last, but not least, one of the most important factors of successful and accurate shooting is self-control. Spotting a squirrel shooting opportunity, switching immediately into 'shooting' mode, calming your breathing, lifting the air rifle steadily and allowing your senses to take over. Once you've shot a few squirrels confidently your mind ... with it's amazing memory ... will take over. Nature has gifted us (and every other living thing) with this tool called *instinct*. Use your instinct. Be confident.

Confidence in your shooting brings success

Health and Safety

I really can't stress enough the importance of safety and vigilance with regard to ownership and handling of a gun. Not only your own safety but also the safety of people around you while it is in your possession ... whether in the field or at home. Don't be fooled into thinking that the humble, low-power air rifle is harmless. We are reminded far too often in the media that the air rifle can kill a human being if it ends up in the wrong hands and is used in an irresponsible circumstances. If you are reading this book it is probably because you either already own an air rifle or intend to own one. Let me state my own rules for staying safe and responsible with an air rifle:

1. Never purchase or use a rifle which doesn't have a safety catch. They lock the trigger and prevent accidental firing of a loaded gun. There is no viable excuse, in this modern era of air rifle technology, for lack of a safety catch. But note point two!

2. Never, ever point a rifle, loaded or unloaded, at anyone or anything you don't intend to shoot. Don't rely on the safety catch preventing an accident in such circumstances. It might fail.

3. Never climb over a gate or cross a barrier while carrying your air rifle. Remove the magazine, clear the barrel then place it safely on the opposite side of the obstacle at a safe distance from you, with the safety catch engaged. Then cross the obstacle, recover the rifle and re-arm it.

Never climb a gate or fence carrying your rifle

4. When travelling ensure the rifle is stored in a rifle slip, unloaded and that the ammunition is distinctly separate from the gun.

5. Never load a magazine into your air rifle until just prior to hunting. After loading, engage the safety catch before setting off. Make checking the safety catch habitual. If you ever raise your rifle to shoot vermin and find the safety catch is already off ... then you've just failed yourself as a responsible and safe shooter.

6. If, while hunting, you encounter anyone else (whether or not they are known to you or they are trespassing) ensure you disarm the air rifle immediately and explain what you're doing. You should never stand and converse with anybody with your rifle armed.

7. Never leave your air rifle unattended while in the field. Even if searching for shot quarry, shoulder the gun and take it with you. As with crossing a barrier, never take your eye off your rifle.

8. When you've finished shooting, before placing the rifle in its slip, cock and fire your rifle into the ground at some distance from you. Now remove the magazine then re-cock and fire again. Make sure your barrel is clear.

9. When back at home (or where-ever you store your gun), ensure that the rifle is immediately secured away. This is important under recently changed legislation around gun security. Don't stop for a coffee or other drink. Lock away your gun first ... preferably in a proper gun-safe. I would always recommend a gun-safe in your house ... even for legal-limit rifles. Children are both naturally curious and devious. Lock your guns away. Please. Remove the risk.

10. Lastly. whenever you have a rifle ... or any gun for that matter ... in your possession, be aware of its capacity for harm. After all, that's why you are carrying it to kill squirrels. Respect it and more importantly, respect the privilege of being deemed a person responsible enough to carry it. For when you do, you represent me ... and the others reading this book. Air rifle hunters.

If you want a complete code of safety for the air rifle, I can highly recommend the British Association for Shooting and Conservation (BASC). I have been a member for many years and their down-loadable guides and codes of practice are easily accessible via their excellent web-site. Membership of BASC, I also give you shooting insurance cover and access to legal advice ... should anything go wrong.

Onto some other Health & Safety considerations. Grey squirrels skulls like walnut kernels, so if you use head shots, never, ever assume a fallen squirrel is dead. Take a long twig to the shot squirrel and rub it over its eyeball. Look for the blink reflex (you can use this trick this with rabbits too). If it blinks, place your muzzle between eye and ear ... point blank ... and finish the job. A numbed, shocked squirrel that suddenly comes alert as you pick it up could bite right through a finger. Just remember its natural diet of acorns nuts and remember how powerful those jaws are!

When handling dead squirrels, I would advise that you carry hygiene wipes or a small bottle of disinfectant gel to clean your hands. Grey squirrels are delvers and diggers, burying and recovering food in woodland soil, which can carry various harmful bacteria. They share tree boughs with pigeons, who can carry salmonella, coccidiosis and other nasty's. Whatever you hunt, personal hygiene should be at a premium until your catch is disposed of (or cooked). There is no evidence that the squirrel parapox virus carried by 70% of the grey squirrel population is seriously harmful to humans. I will say though that I had succumbed to several uncomfortable eye infections prior to reviewing my handling of dead squirrels. Since I adopted a robust hygiene routine, I haven't one infection.

Squirrels can carry a host of bacteria picked up from the soil or bough

Squirrel Sign

There are many give-away clues to the presence of grey squirrels in woodland and most are usually feeding sign. Feeding sign such as chewed fir cones or maize cobs can identify the culprit. Those little, dexterous paws can turn a cob or pine cone easily and the cast-away remnant looks the same as when we eat a pear. Squirrels use natural 'tables' such as tree stumps to sit and eat nuts, eggs or maize. Shredded hazel nuts or sweet chestnuts on the forest floor may be noticed too. If you find empty, gnawed hazel nut kernels then you've found squirrel territory. Signs of shallow digging on the woodland floor are also a sure sign of a nearby drey ... even if you can't see it. Greys will recover cached nuts and seeds over the winter and leave small excavations. Other sign may include gnawed out bird boxes (after egg raiding). Squirrel prints are very distinctive in snow (like a tiny rabbits) and in mud (due to the claws).

Gnawed hazel nut kernels and a chewed maize cob

Chewed out bird box and squirrel prints in wet mud

Hunting Tips and Hints

The first and most important thing to say is here is that the purpose of grey squirrel control is to help save forestry and reclaim breeding ground for the red squirrel. If you are lucky enough (I'm not) to live in an area where reds are breeding, knowing how to identify the red from the grey squirrel is essential. To shoot a red squirrel (even in error) is a wildlife crime. Never, ever take a shot at a squirrel (or any creature for that matter) unless you can positively identify it. The main feature that identifies the mature red squirrel is it's pointed, tufted ears (the greys are small and rounded). Yet young reds with undeveloped ears and immature fur can look (in silhouette) very like a young grey squirrel. Vice versa, the grey squirrel (particularly in spring and early summer) often has splashes of russet fur down its back and can look slightly red! Before you dare point a gun at a squirrel, please do your homework.

The squirrels survival instinct is an inherent part of its attraction as a hunting quarry but makes chasing them with an air rifle pretty futile. You need a static target. My preferred way to target grey squirrels is through ambushing them. Simply find those highways, pick the right times of day, wait patiently or stalk very slowly and you will get good bags of greys. You don't particularly need military style camouflage or hides either. You just need stealth and shadow. In summer months, the perfect time to hunt greys is an hour after dawn or an hour before dusk when they use the coolness to forage. The squirrels will avoid heat and humidity and take to the shade of the dreys in warm weather. In winter, they are best hunted during the middle of the day, when the sun has warmed the dreys and they venture out to feed or breed. In winter, of course, they are much more visible (as are the dreys themselves).

Shooting squirrels can be at a premium on what I call 'rainbow' days. Days with intermittent sunshine and showers. Grey squirrels aren't partial to rain and will lie up in the drey during showers but as soon as the warmth of the sun hits the drey, they will scamper out to feed. At any time of day. Staking out natural feeding tables can be fruitful, though you might have a long wait. Those stumps and fallen boughs in the wood covered in shredded and splintered nut kernels. Any one squirrel could use several of these, however .. so visits are random. The squirrel is a lone feeder, so don't expect to see several on one of these natural tables. That only seems to happen on garden bird tables. Shooting greys on bird tables is always tempting but is a practice I usually refuse to undertake when asked by householders or landowners. My reasoning is simple, killing activity around a bird table will scare away the birds for a good time. Particularly if blood is spilt on the table itself. No, I prefer to ambush the greys on their way to and from the feeders if I can.

I mentioned the six week gestation period earlier? Well, that obviously means the grey squirrel will mate roughly six weeks before February or July. During December and May, I'm on the lookout for squirrel mating activity. Squirrels are extremely vulnerable, chasing up and down trunks or along the woodland floor, playing out their 'catch-me-if-you-can' rituals. They are so focused (the females on flirting and the males on pursuit) that they are often oblivious to the watching hunter. I've even had squirrels run across my boots while standing in grey squirrel mating territory. A loud hiss, the click of your tongue or the waggle of a Primos call (see below) will bring them alert. They are also vulnerable to a shot while pinned against a trunk catching their breath.

The grey squirrel mating chase

I shoot squirrels all year around but there is no doubt that winter is the ideal time to thin out greys, when the leaf canopy has dropped and they are at their most exposed. On cool, misty mornings when the dew-drops hang on the branches above, squirrels expose their presence with their motion causing tiny audible cascades from the canopy. Likewise, after heavy snow, their movement above will cause small avalanches to fall to the floor, exposing their position to the shooter.

If a squirrel spots you (or your dog) and perches on a bough hissing, chattering and flicking its tail, its probably a juvenile. Fully mature greys tend not to do this ... experience lending itself to flight rather than fight. If you hear this classic warning signal but can't see the squirrel, you will find it hard to identify where the sound is coming from. The grey squirrel seems to 'throw' its voice as cleverly as the magpie does. Be patient and stay where you are ... because that little 'hissy-fit' means it can see you and involves that flickering of its bushy tail. If the animal can see you, you will eventually see it too. If you have a dog with you, it may be reacting to that ... so move quietly to where the dog is and look about again.

The squirrels eye position is much like that of the rabbit and hare. Placed on the sides of its head, the eyes give nearly, but not quite, 360 degree vision. It's blind spot is directly ahead so a squirrel scampering along the ground, towards you, might not see you even if you are in the middle of a woodland ride. Simply squat slowly to shrink your outline and click your tongue loudly. It will halt in its tracks, allowing you to shoot. If it runs for a tree, be ready. Most squirrels will stop within fifteen feet from the ground to check for danger. High enough to avoid a ground predator like a fox or dog but low enough to evaluate any aerial threat.

One thing I would like to beg from the reader. Please don't get tempted into the 'drey shooting' antics I see used by many shot-gunners at winter. This form of squirrel control has no place in a *sensible hunters agenda ... even with a 12 gauge gun. It* cannot guarantee a clean kill within the fortress of the drey and the drey may actually be inhabited by something like a long-eared owl, which often use old dreys to nest. The single pellet fired blindly from an air rifle into a drey is most unlikely to kill, only maim if it makes contact. There is, however, a useful technique which draws on this without the risk of indiscriminate injury of either grey squirrels or other innocent inhabitants of a drey. Using a multi-shot PCP air rifle, you can shoot a pellet or two into a bough to disrupt the occupants. This will often convince squirrels to exit the drey. Use a couple of loud clicks of the tongue as they escape to make them stop still for a shot. Sometimes it works, more often it doesn't, but it's safe and sporting. The other way is to move them out of the dreys using a slingshot, which is also great fun!

Author using a slingshot to disturb a drey

The best way to stalk a small wood for squirrels is to enter it at the lee (windless) side and work in diagonal sweeps across the wind. The breeze must always be in your face. Any squirrels that spot you will be driven to the far end of the copse.

Like many mammals, grey squirrels include fungi in their diet and they are particularly fond of Fly Agaric, which is toxic to humans. If you spot a patch of this stunning red mushroom on your shooting ground, keep an eye on it.

Another trick used by shooters and photographers to attract squirrels into range is to tie an old deer antler to a tree trunk below a drey. The grey squirrel likes to hone its chiselled teeth on cast antlers, probably also drawing calcium and other nutrients from them.

Squirrels, like most wild creatures, can be 'called' within range. They are naturally curious but they are also very suspicious. Mimicking he sound of another squirrel needs to be authentic to attract greys and I favour the Primos 'Squirrel Buster' which allows a variety of calls once you master it. I would recommend that you watch video demos of how to use it properly on You Tube, such as this one.   https://www.youtube.com/watch?v=kftO3gW5tVA

The Primos 'Squirrel Buster' ... a useful critter caller

The Squirrel Hunters Dog

Despite the fact that under current law you can't let your dog chase and kill squirrels, the use of a dog when squirrel shooting can give considerable advantage. My lurcher, Dylan, and I have accounted for thousands of grey squirrels over the past 10 years. He does the sensory work. The millions of olfactory receptors in his wet nose can pick up squirrel scent from fifty yards away. His ears work like radar dishes to pick up sound and he can sense an incoming grey from a hundred yards away ... long before I can see or here it. Over the years, his experience has developed to anticipate the behaviour of a hunted grey and to understand his part in the game. That is to say, he locates or alerts me to greys and I cull them. He understands that. His job is also to retrieve or, if necessary (and it does happen) deliver a swift dispatch if my shot isn't clean. Ninety nine percent of the time he only has to retrieve but he can get into briar patches and scrub to locate a dead squirrel, making my life much easier. Most importantly, he loves the hunt. He exists for it and though we hunt other species like rats and rabbits, he is in his element on grey squirrels.

Dylan retrieving a shot squirrel

So ... how do you train a dog to work to the squirrel rifle? This book isn't the place for a full blown dog training missive (instead see my book, The Hunters Hound). The most important thing to teach with squirrels are the 'stay' and 'leave' commands. I teach these long before a dog is allowed to hunt with me. To be able to station your hound and trust it to stay in position is vital to the air rifle stalker. Once quarry is located, you want the dog to take a passive stance while you execute the shot. A dog careering about will keep your quarry on the move and you need it static for the shot. Similarly, you must break the dog from exercising its natural chasing urge, unless you permit it to do so. Hence the 'leave' command. This discipline, vital when working around stock and poultry on farms, once taught can be easily transferred to apply to squirrels and other quarry. The rifleman's dog, unlike the coursers, needs to understand that the kill is delivered by the gun. Much of the initial training done with a pup to secure this discipline and trust of your dog will be done using a long lead and constant praise and reward. You will check the chasing pup using the 'leave' command until it associates 'leave' with stopping chasing immediately. As the pup develops, you will use associative training to pre-empt the chase and utter 'leave' as soon as you see the dog eyeing a chicken, the farmyard cat or a running pheasant. This is hugely challenging, as the dogs natural urge is to chase, but it is achievable and a crucial discipline in a rifle hunters canine companion.

Not only can a dog track scent on trails and rides but they can play 'second man' to drive squirrels around a trunk back into your line of fire. A hunted squirrel will often hide on the opposite side of a tree trunk, out of your sight. A trained dog like my Dylan can be sent to the opposite side of the tree and its movement will force the grey (which will always react to the most immediate, moving threat it perceives) back to your side of the tree. Just make sure you are standing back far enough to engage the squirrel in your scope and execute the shot.

A perfect woodland companion

Recycling Your Squirrels

How you decide to recycle your shot squirrels may depend on how a proposed National cull is prescribed by the authorities. If proof is needed via a tail count, you will need to know how to prepare tails for storage. This is a useful skill to learn anyway as if the Government don't want them, many fly-fishermen and fly-fishing outlets will. The hairs from the bushy tail make for great filaments on home-made flies. I'll explain how to prepare a tail later.

The first method I'll discuss is whole carcase disposal, assuming you don't want to use your catch more productively. There is a lot of nonsense written on official advice pages (yes, I'm talking Government or similar) about incinerating squirrel corpses, deep burying them or wrapping them and placing them in domestic waste bins. The best way to recycle a whole squirrel which you don't want to use is to put it back into 'the circle of life'. If you leave fresh corpses outside fox dens or badger setts and just cut a slice through the gut to release the scent I will guarantee you they will have been cleaned away by the next morning. If you have reservations about feeding foxes or badgers, just consider this? You have probably just saved a couple of pheasant poults or chickens as their predator is less hungry. Which is why I often leave grey squirrel corpses on a particular midden (muck) pile on one of my shooting permissions where the buzzards collect them. They even follow me at times, expecting a treat and are rarely let down! Hopefully, it keeps their eyes of the young game-birds for a day or two.

OK ... let's assume you just want the tail for reasons described above. The temptation is to just cut it off, which I do only if I have an immediate recipient for the brush. If it needs to be stored, perhaps frozen or posted you need to approach this differently as you need to remove the tail bone before the flesh that surrounds it starts to putrefy. I use a self-discovered tool for this, which is a clothes peg (see the photos below). Cut a nick around the base of the tail, ensuring you don't cut into the flesh and bone itself. All you want to do is separate the tail skin from the main body skin. Ease the tail fur back up towards the tip of the tail just a centimetre. Place the peg across the exposed skin (as though pegging a clothes line), grip the peg tightly and pull away from the body in one smooth motion. This will draw the tail off the tail muscle.

Skinning squirrels is just as easy and can be done in less than a minute with practise. Place the corpse belly down, back legs akimbo. Lift the tail to expose the area between tail and anus. Use a sharp knife to make a slit in the outer skin, drawing the knife across to each rear hip. Try not to cut into the flesh. This should now create a flap at the base of the tail. Flip the animal over to lay the tail on the floor. Put the heel of your boot on the tail and flap. Grasping the back legs tightly, draw upwards sharply and you will strip the upper body. Now hold the animal by the head and strip off the 'trousers' … the rear legs … with a sharp tug. Now is the time to remove the head with a sharp knife and to gut the carcase. Slice through the belly skin, ensuring you don't penetrate the paunch (just as with rabbits). Holding the squirrel by the head, place a couple of fingers into the void and pull out the innards, heart, lungs and kidneys. You now have a kitchen-ready carcase which just needs washing and jointing. Please note, I always use disposable gloves for field preparation like this (see Health & Safety). Again here, I am going to refer you to a very good You Tube video which shows you the method described above:

https://www.youtube.com/watch?v=4c8OyexZ10E

A good crop of greys

Squirrel Recipes

Squirrels, even more so than chickens, are very healthy eaters themselves. Living primarily on high protein foods such as nuts and fruits (supplemented with egg and meat in the right season) they are a clean meat. The problem, for me, is the lack of content! A plump rabbit carries about six times more edible meat than a squirrel. As the sage said, 'never look a gift-horse in the mouth'. The grey squirrel is abundant, edible and (I write this before a cull) considered a delicacy now in many respectable restaurants. Generally any recipe for rabbit can be used to cook squirrel. As I write this treatise, some restaurants are paying up to £5 per squirrel (unfortunately, not near me!). You, though, can eat for the price of a few air gun pellets so here are a couple of very simple recipes:

Chilli Squirrel
(Serves Four)

I have to confess I don't eat a lot of squirrel and perhaps I should eat more. My preference, as described earlier, is to contra-feed other predators to relax pressure on game birds and songbirds. However, when I do eat them I like to use the meat as a base for a spicier or more exotic dish ... as you would with chicken. This recipe is an easy way to 'sexy-up' squirrel meat.

Prime saddle and haunch meat from 4 squirrels, diced.
One tablespoon sunflower oil.
1 tin chopped tomatoes.
1 tin red kidney beans.
1 large onion, chopped.
One tablespoon hot chilli powder.
Half teaspoon garlic salt.
Couple of pinches of black pepper.
Two cup fulls of easy-cook rice.
Garlic baguette.
Fresh parsley.

Heat the sunflower oil on a large wok and stir fry the squirrel meat, adding the garlic salt and black pepper. When lightly browned, stir in the chopped onion until soft. Tip in the chopped tomatoes, kidney beans and chilli powder, adding half a tin of water (use the tomato tin). Bring to a simmer, stirring all the time, then turn down low and simmer for about half an hour. Heat the oven for the garlic baguette and pop it in about ten minutes before serving. At the same time, boil four cupfuls of water in a large pan and add the rice. Simmer for ten minutes, ensuring it doesn't dry out. Drain and serve the rice in a circle on the plates, spoon the chilli into the centre, adding a sprig or two of parsley to dress. Cut and serve the garlic baguette on a separate dish.

Bourguignon Carolinensis
(Serves four - slow cooker recipe)

This is a lush winter Sunday supper. If, like me, you are too busy to eat during the day then the slow-cooker is the perfect compromise. I love cooking. I find it as relaxing as hunting or photography. This is the sort of meal I will throw together after a mornings hunting so that it brews while I get on with writing and processing photo's for an article. The smell emanating from the slow cooker inspires me. When we dish it and eat it, it tires me. Work first, supper later. The perfect Sunday evening.

Prime saddle and haunch meat from 4 squirrels, diced.
1 large onion, chopped.
1 large carrot, diced.
1 sweet red pepper, sliced.
Half-punnet button mushrooms, sliced.
Half teaspoon garlic salt.
Couple of pinches of black pepper.
1 Bourguignon packet sauce (Schwartz, Colmans, or similar).
Glass red wine.
250ml cold water.
2lb potatoes.
Yorkshire puddings.
Garden peas.

This is easy, once you've chopped the meat and diced the vegetables. Drink half of the glass of red wine and just throw the other half into the cook-pot with everything except the potatoes, Yorkshire puddings and peas. Cook on low for six hours, lidded. Approximately forty five minutes before you dish, warm the oven for the puddings and prepare a pan of water for the potatoes and another for the peas. You know the rest! Mash the potatoes before serving up with the puddings and peas, spooning the Bourguignon across the lot. Delicious!

Bibliography

'Squirrels In Britain', Keith Laidler, David & Charles 1980.

Rural Development Service Technical Advice Note 09

Airgun Fieldcraft: A Lifetimes Hunting Advice. Ian Barnett. Blaze Publishing.

About The Author

Ian Barnett is a freelance country sports writer and photographer based in Norfolk, UK.
Ian has hunted with air guns and lurchers for forty years and writes regularly for Airgun Shooter and The Countryman's Weekly about hunting and field-craft. He is also a keen wildlife and landscape photographer. Many of Ian's images can be seen on his Wildscribbler photo website:

http://www.wildscribbler.co.uk

As well as many hundreds of magazine articles, Ian has several published books to his credit including:

The Airgun Hunter's Year
Airgun Fieldcraft
The Hunter's Way
The Hunter's Hound
Jaguar! (a novel)

Ian also writes a regular countryside blog on his website, which also details how to purchase his books:

http://www.wildscribbler.com

Printed in Great Britain
by Amazon.co.uk, Ltd.,
Marston Gate.